TWEETABLE
ABRAHAM LINCOLN

Infotainment Press

Tweetable Abraham Lincoln: Quips, Quotes & Other One-Liners

Copyright © 2021 by Infotainment Press

All rights reserved. No portion of this book may be reproduced, stored in a retrieval system, or transmitted in any form or by any means—electronic, mechanical, photocopy, recording, scanning, or other—except for brief quotations in critical reviews or articles, without the prior written permission of the publisher.

TWEETABLE ABRAHAM LINCOLN

QUIPS, QUOTES & OTHER ONE-LINERS

There is an important sense in which government
   is distinctive from administration . . .
   government is perpetual.

We cannot elect extreme men.

Military glory—that attractive rainbow, that rises
   in showers of blood—that serpent's eye,
   that charms to destroy.

But I must say I have a great respect for the semicolon;
   it's a useful little chap.

It is easier to pay a large sum than it is to pay
   a larger one.

You must judge which class those belong to whom you meet; I leave it to you to determine from the facts.

I also acknowledge your rights and my obligations, under the constitution, in regard to slaves.

Habeas Corpus, does not discharge men who are proved to be guilty of defined crime.

There has never been but one question . . . how to keep a few men from saying to many men: You work and earn bread and we will eat it.

Excellence in any undertaking can be found in details that most people barely notice, but those who know, know.

I hold that, as a general rule, the commander in the field is the better judge of the necessity in any particular case.

Inside this portal dwells new strength in the security, serenity, and radiance of those I love above life itself.

We must not promise what we ought not, lest we be called on to perform what we cannot.

A blind horse upon a treadmill is a perfect illustration of what a laborer should be— all the better for being blind.

I am very little inclined on any occasion to say anything unless I hope to produce some good by it.

I think the authors of that notable instrument [Declaration of Independence] intended to include all men.

*T*hat some achieve great success, is proof to all that others can achieve it as well.

*P*ublic opinion, though often formed upon a wrong basis, yet generally has a strong underlying sense of justice.

*W*hen you return to your homes, rise up to the height of a generation of men worthy of a free government.

*I*n very truth he was, the noblest work of God—an honest man.

In this country, one can scarcely be so poor, that, if he will, he can acquire sufficient education to get through the world respectably.

I understand that it is a maxim of law, that a poor plea may be a good plea to a bad declaration.

I wish to assure you, as once a friend, and still, I hope, not an enemy.

If you would win a man to your cause, first convince him that you are his sincere friend.

Let the people know the truth and the country will be safe.

Through their deeds, the dead of battle have spoken more eloquently for themselves than any of the living ever could.

Nevertheless, amid the greatest difficulties of my Administration, I would place my whole reliance on God.

Presidents and Kings are not apt to see flaws in their own arguments.

A lawyer's time and advice are his stock in trade.

Can treaties be more faithfully enforced between aliens than laws can among friends?

The friends I left that parting day, how changed as time has sped. Young childhood grown, strong manhood gray, and half of all are dead.

I consider the central idea pervading this struggle is the necessity of proving that popular government is not an absurdity.

As a nation, we began by declaring that all men are created equal.

I am a firm believer in the people.

Women are the only people I am afraid of who I never thought would hurt me.

Capital is only the fruit of labor, and could never have existed if labor had not first existed.

I shall never sink the rights of mankind to the malice, wrong, or avarice of another's wishes, in the relation of client and attorney.

Without the assistance of that divine being, I cannot succeed. With that assistance I cannot fail.

It is easier to pay any sum when we are able than it is to pay it before we are able.

I don't believe in a law to prevent a man from getting rich; it would do more harm than good.

If you wish to be a lawyer, attach no consequence to the place you are in, or the person you are with.

War at the best, is terrible, and this war of ours, in its magnitude and in its duration, is one of the most terrible.

I shall be a humble instrument in the hands of the Almighty.

Let the constitution become the political religion of the nation.

Discourage litigation. Persuade your neighbors to compromise whenever you can.

The world is agreed that labor is the source from which human wants are mainly supplied.

I believe that people should fight for what they believe and only what they believe.

It is for us the living, rather, to be dedicated here to the unfinished work which they who fought here have thus far so nobly advanced.

Standing as a unit among yourselves, you can, directly, and indirectly, bribe enough of our men to carry the day.

The man does not live who is more devoted to peace than I am. None who would do more to preserve it.

The Dred Scott decision helped to carry an election, and then was kicked to the winds.

Never stir up litigation. A worse man can scarcely be found than one who does this.

If I find a venomous snake lying on the open prairie, I seize the first stick and kill him at once.

A friend is one who has the same enemies as you have.

It is a delicate matter to oppose the wishes of a friend.

If not hindered, the man who says nothing is sure to help the enemy.

With the catching end the pleasures of the chase.

And then, there will be some black men who can remember they have helped mankind on to this great consummation.

If this is coffee, please bring me some tea; but if this is tea, please bring me some coffee.

Important principles may and must be inflexible.

The assurance conveyed by this high compliment, [honorary degree] is most grateful to me.

Every man over forty is responsible for his face.

I don't like to hear cut and dried sermons. No—when I hear a man preach, I like to see him act as if he were fighting bees.

Let him patiently wait for the fruit to ripen and the ripe pear at length falls into his lap.

The severest justice may not always be the best policy.

I never did like to work, and I don't deny it. I'd rather read, tell stories, crack jokes, talk, laugh—anything but work.

It seemed to me that the blue jay was trying to communicate with me . . . "What?! What?!" I would yell back, but he never did speak English.

The negative principle that no law is free law, is not much known except among lawyers.

I am thankful to God for this approval of the people.

Nothing will divert me from my purpose.

I have stepped out upon this platform that I may see you and you see me, and in the arrangement I have the best of the bargain.

*I*n such suggestions by me, quite likely very little will be new to you, and a large part of the rest possibly already known to be erroneous.

*I*n my poor, lean, lank face nobody has ever seen that any cabbages were sprouting out.

*A*ll men are created free and equal.

*A*ll that I am or ever hope to be, I owe to my angel mother.

Some single mind must be master, else there will be no agreement in anything.

Now we are told in advance, the government shall be broken up, unless we surrender to those we have beaten, before we take the offices.

Our adversaries over the way attempted to appropriate it ["Dixie"], but I insisted that we fairly captured it.

It may be remarked: First, that we had the same constitution then, as now.

To the best of my judgment I have labored for, and not against the Union.

Whenever you shall have conquered all resistance to the Union, if I shall urge you to continue fighting.

We are met on a great battle-field of that war. We have come to dedicate a portion of that field, as a final resting place.

Has it not got down as thin as the homeopathic soup that was made by boiling the shadow of a pigeon?

Only events and not a man's exertions in his own behalf, can make a President.

He who would be no slave, must consent to have no slave.

It is difficult to make a man miserable while he feels worthy of himself and claims kindred to the great God who made him.

Believing everyone is dangerous, but believing nobody is more dangerous.

Every man has a mouth to be fed and two hands with which to feed it and that bread should be allowed to go to that mouth.

It is an established maxim in morals that he who makes an assertion without knowing whether it is true or false, is guilty of falsehood.

Neither party anticipated that the cause of the conflict might cease with, or even before, the conflict itself should cease.

These [the armed forces] are not our reliance against a resumption of tyranny in our fair land.

The slaveholder does not like to be considered a mean fellow, and hence he has to argue himself into the belief that slavery is right.

Let us judge not that we be not judged. The prayers of both could not be answered; that of neither has been answered fully.

The past is the cause of the present, and the present will be the cause of the future.

Soldiers, I bid you God-speed to your homes.

I am slow to learn and slow to forget that which I have learned.

I did say that I do wish to see the spread of slavery arrested.

My first impulse would be to free all the slaves.

The democracy of today hold the liberty of one man to be absolutely nothing.

Whenever I hear anyone arguing for slavery, I feel a strong impulse to see it tried on him personally.

It is impossible to destroy it [constitiution], except by some action not provided for in the instrument itself.

Honor also to the citizen who cares for his brother in the field.

No country can sustain, in idleness, more than a small percentage of its numbers.

The people when rightly and fully trusted will return the trust.

The constitution is not in its application in all respects, the same.

Do not destroy that immortal emblem of humanity, the Declaration of Independence.

If we could first know where we are, and whither we are tending, we could then better judge what to do, and how to do it.

Whether the owners of this species of property [slavery] do really see it as it is, it is not for me to say.

My own wisdom and that of all about me seemed insufficient for that day.

You cannot escape this conclusion; and yet, are you willing to abide by it?

I do blame those, whoever they may be, who falsely put such a charge in circulation against me.

When the Know Nothings get control, it will read "all men are created equal except [African Americans], foreigners, and Catholics."

Anybody will do for you, but not for me. I must have somebody.

And at the outset, I am glad to see that a system of labor prevails in New England under which laborers can strike when they want to.

Educated people must labor. Otherwise, education itself would become a positive and intolerable evil.

What is to be will be, and no prayers of ours can reverse the decree.

Slavery is wrong in its effect upon white people and free labor; it is the only thing that threatens the Union.

Politics, as a trade, finds most and leaves nearly all dishonest.

It is not merely for today, but for all time to come that we should perpetuate for our children's children this great and free government.

Forget that you have anyone to fall back upon, and you will do justice to yourself and your client.

The dogmas of the quiet past are inadequate to the stormy present.

Always bear in mind that our own resolution to succeed is more important than any one thing.

Mammoth farms are like tools or weapons, which are too heavy to be handled.

Let us then turn this government back into the channel in which the framers of the Constitution originally placed it.

You can lose everything in life, but not dreams.

Our safety, our liberty, depends upon preserving the Constitution of the United States as our fathers made it inviolate.

I fully appreciate the present peril the country is in, and the weight of responsibility on me.

And having thus chosen our course, without guile, and with pure purpose, let us renew our trust in God.

I like to see a man proud of the place in which he lives. I like to see a man live so that his place will be proud of him.

My father taught me to work, but not to love it.

In giving freedom to the slave, we assure freedom to the free—honorable alike in what we give, and what we preserve.

Passion has helped us; but can do so no more. It will in future be our enemy.

The philosophy of the schoolroom in one generation is the philosophy of government in the next.

Seriously, I do not think I am fit for the presidency.

There is not a more fatal error to young lawyers than relying too much on speech-making.

Gentlemen, why do you not laugh? With the fearful strain that is upon me day and night, if I did not laugh, I should die.

Fondly do we hope, fervently do we pray, that this mighty scourge of war may speedily pass away.

It is easiest to be all things to all men, but it is not honest. Self respect must be sacrificed every hour in the day.

The Union is much older than the Constitution.

The principles of Jefferson are the definitions and axioms of free society.

My concern is not whether God is on our side; my greatest concern is to be on God's side, for God is always right.

If once you forfeit the confidence of your fellow-citizens, you can never regain their respect and esteem.

Thanks to all. For the great republic—for the principle it lives by, and keeps alive—for man's vast future—thanks to all.

You cannot fail, if you resolutely determine, that you will not.

I have always wanted to deal with everyone I meet candidly and honestly.

I think that one of the causes of these failures is that our best and greatest men have greatly underestimated the size of this question.

Few can be induced to labor exclusively for posterity, and none will do it enthusiastically.

What is conservatism? Is it not the adherence to the old and tried against the new and untried?

I do order and declare that all persons held as slaves henceforward shall be free.

*T*he inclination to share thoughts with one another is probably an original impulse of our nature.

*O*ne-sixth, and a little more, of the population of the United States are slaves looked upon as property, as nothing but property.

*I*t is both curious and interesting that those opposed to Jefferson should now be celebrating his birthday.

*P*eace will come soon and come to stay, and so come as to be worth keeping in all future time.

The proposition that there is a struggle between the white man and the [black man] contains a falsehood. There is no struggle.

Law is nothing else but the best reason of wise men applied for ages to the transactions and business of mankind.

Take all that you can of this book upon reason, and the balance on faith, and you will live and die a happier man.

Kindness is the only service that will stand the storm of life and not wash out.

Those who think it [slavery] right, of course will look upon the rattlesnake as a jewel, and call the wren an ornament.

The shepherd drives the wolf from the sheep's throat, for which the sheep thanks the shepherd as a liberator.

Thinking [slavery] right, they are justified in asking its protection; thinking it wrong, we cannot consent to vote for it.

He can compress the most words into the smallest ideas of any man I ever met.

I must stand with anybody that stands right, and stand with him while he is right, and part with him when he goes wrong.

I have no other [ambition] so great as that of being truly esteemed of my fellow men.

*T*hose who shall have tasted actual freedom I believe can never be slaves, or quasi slaves again.

*B*oth parties deprecated war, but one of them would make war rather than let the nation survive.

*W*hoever molds public sentiment goes deeper than he who enacts statutes, or pronounces judicial decisions.

My mind is like a piece of steel, very hard to scratch anything on it and almost impossible after you get it there to rub it out.

I believe in the Providence of the most men, the largest purse, and the longest cannon.

I agree with you, Mr. Chairman, that the working men are the basis of all governments.

He was arrested because he was damaging the army . . . upon which the nation depends.

I am in favor of animal rights as well as human rights. That is the way of a whole human being.

No, if destruction be our lot we must ourselves be its author and finisher. As a nation of free men we will live forever or die by suicide.

Now be it understood that I do not pretend to know all about the matter. I am merely going to speculate a little about some of its phases.

Continue to execute all the express provisions of our national constitution, and the Union will endure forever.

The true rule for the Military is to seize such property as is needed for Military uses and reasons, and let the rest alone.

When men are framing a supreme law and chart of government, they use language as short and direct and plain as can be found.

Let no eye but your own see this—not that there is anything wrong, or even ungenerous in it; but it would be misconstrued.

America will never be destroyed from the outside. If we falter and lose our freedoms, it will be because we destroyed ourselves.

There we should in every way resist it as a wrong, treating it as a wrong, with the fixed idea that it must and will come to an end.

We cannot act otherwise than we do, believing that slavery is wrong.

God bless all the churches and blessed be to God, who, in this our great trial, giveth us the churches.

The way of democracy began to see the wisdom and justice of it.

Not one of these Democrats can show that he said that five years ago.

You distinguish between yourself and my original friends—a distinction which, by your leave, I propose to forget.

Money will cease to be master and will then become servant of humanity.

These men ask for just the same thing, fairness, and fairness only.

In all that people can individually do as well for themselves, government ought not to interfere.

The prayers of both could not be answered; that of neither has been answered fully.

And now, beware of rashness. Beware of rashness, but with energy, and sleepless vigilance, go forward, and give us victories.

A house divided against itself cannot stand. I believe this government cannot endure, permanently half slave and half free.

Achievement has no color.

You know I dislike slavery; and you fully admit the abstract wrong of it.

It is certain that thorough cultivation would spare half or more than half, the cost of land.

Whatever you are, be a good one.

The truth is, that this question [slavery] is one of national importance, and we cannot help dealing with it: we must do something about it.

You cannot have the right to do what is wrong!

The worst thing you can do for those you love is the things they could and should do themselves.

Let us at all times remember that all American citizens are brothers of a common country.

Don't stir them up to anger.

Yet the contest began, And, having begun He could give the final victory to either side any day. Yet the contest proceeds.

If you are resolutely determined to make a lawyer of yourself, the thing is more than half done already.

To ease another's heartache is to forget one's own.

Thoughtful men must feel that the fate of civilization upon this continent is involved in the issue of our contest.

You cannot escape the responsibility of tomorrow by evading it today.

Human nature is the same—people at the South are the same as those at the North, barring the difference in circumstances.

Extemporaneous speaking . . . is the lawyer's avenue to the public.

I think it is enough if the man does no wrong hereafter.

No country can sustain, in idleness, more than a small percentage of its numbers. The great majority must labor at something productive.

If the end brings me out wrong, ten angels swearing I was right would make no difference.

Property is the fruit of labor; property is desirable, is a positive good in the world.

You need not be told that persisting in a charge which one does not know to be true is simply malicious slander.

No matter how much the cats fight, there always seem to be plenty of kittens.

Every blade of grass is a study; and to produce two, where there was but one, is both a profit and a pleasure.

I do not impugn the motives of anyone opposed to me.

The sharpness of a refusal or the edge of a rebuke may be blunted by an appropriate story.

A husband and wife may be divorced, and go out of the presence and reach of each other, but our country cannot do this.

I also believe you do not mix politics with your profession, in which you are right.

Laughter can be used to soothe the mind and get rid of those awful thoughts.

What once has happened, will invariably happen again.

Happy day, when, all appetites controlled, all poisons subdued, all matter subjected, mind, all conquering mind, shall live.

He who does something at the head of one Regiment, will eclipse him who does nothing at the head of a hundred.

Get books, sit yourself down anywhere, and go to reading them yourself.

He who dissuades one man from volunteering, or induces one soldier to desert, weakens the Union cause.

But soberly, it is now no child's play to save
the principles of Jefferson from total overthrow
in this nation.

If he screams when whipped, they say it is not caused
by the pains he suffers, but he screams because we
instigate him to outcrying.

They have constantly brought forward small cures for
great sores—plasters too small to cover the wound.

The financing of all public enterprise, and
the conduct of the treasury will become matters
of practical administration.

We have, as all will agree, a free Government, where every man has a right to be equal with every other man.

A "don't care" policy won't prevail, for everybody does care.

Intelligence, patriotism, Christianity; firm reliance on Him, are still competent to adjust, in the best way, all our present difficulty.

A limb must be amputated to save a life, but a life is never given wisely to save a limb.

We can complain because rose bushes have thorns, or rejoice because thorn bushes have roses.

It is safe to assert that no government proper ever had a provision in its organic law for its own termination.

You do not want to hear of it from the pulpit because it is not a religion.

Prior to my installation here it had been inculcated that any State had a lawful right to secede from the national Union.

Stand with anyone that is right; stand with him while he is right and part with him when he goes wrong.

We should be too big to take offense and too noble to give it.

The war will cease on the part of the government, whenever it shall have ceased on the part of those who began it.

The way is plain, peaceful, generous, just—a way which, if followed, the world will forever applaud, and God must forever bless.

Their "Union" contrivances are not for us, for they reverse the scriptural order and call the righteous, not sinners to repentance.

The government should create, issue, and circulate all the currency and credit needed to satisfy the spending power of the government.

It [the slavery question] attaches to the body politic as much and as closely as the natural wants attach to our natural bodies.

We believe—nay, we know, that slavery is the only thing that has ever threatened the perpetuity of the Union itself.

The demon of intemperance ever seems to have delighted in sucking the blood of genius and of generosity.

The probability that we may fail in the struggle ought not to deter us from the support of a cause we believe to be just.

How many legs does a dog have if you call the tail a leg? Four. Calling a tail a leg doesn't make it a leg.

I much fear that the spirit which you have aided to infuse into the Army will now turn upon you.

I see the storm coming, and I know that his hand is in it. If He has a place and work for me—and I think He has—I believe I am ready.

I bite my lip and keep quiet.

Such will be a great lesson of peace; teaching men that what they cannot take by an election, neither can they take by a war.

You have to do your own growing, no matter how tall your grandfather was.

Books serve to show a man that those original thoughts of his aren't very new after all.

We hold to no doctrines, and make no declarations, which were not held to and made by our fathers who framed the Government.

How weak and fruitless must be any word of mine.

What remains undone demands our most sincere prayers to, and reliance upon, Him, without whom, all human effort is vain.

If slavery is right, all words, acts, laws, and constitutions against it should be silenced and swept away.

For every [Union] soldier enslaved by the enemy or sold into slavery, a rebel soldier shall be placed at hard labor.

You cannot strengthen the weak by weakening the strong.

I have no interest in a thing which has the power of making me miserable.

I believe I have made some marks which will tell for the cause of civil liberty long after I am gone.

Destroy this spirit and you have planted the seeds of despotism around your own doors.

It is a certain truth, that you can enter, and graduate in, Harvard University; and having made the attempt, you must succeed in it.

Let us do our duty, but let us look to what our duty is, and do nothing except after due deliberation.

It is at least more unusual nowadays to find a man who can hold his tongue than to find one who cannot.

A prohibition law strikes a blow at the very principles upon which our government was founded.

Man was made for immortality.

It is a quality of revolutions not to go by old times or old laws; but to break up both, and make new ones.

Work, work, work, is the main thing.

To remain as I am is impossible; I must die or be better, it appears to me.

Let us not be slandered from our duties, or intimidated from preserving our dignity and our rights by any menace.

What kills a skunk is the publicity it gives itself.

In great contests each party claims to act in accordance with the will of God.

Fellow-citizens, we cannot escape history.

Almost everything, especially of governmental policy, is an inseparable compound of evil and good.

There's no honorable way to kill, no gentle way to destroy. There is nothing good in war. Except its ending.

I know that the Lord is always on the side of the right.

They [laborers] are not obliged to work under all circumstances, and are not tied down and obliged to labor whether you pay them or not!

If I had had my way, this war would never have been commenced.

In law it is a good policy to never plead what you need not, lest you oblige yourself to prove what you can not.

I am a slow walker, but I never walk back.

Broken by it, I too, may be; bow to it I never will.

Understanding the spirit of our institutions to aim at the elevation of men, I am opposed to whatever tends to degrade them.

My Best Friend is a person who will give me a book I have not read.

I take the official oath today with no mental reservations; no purpose to construe the Constitution by any hypercritical rules.

Knavery and flattery are blood relations.

I cannot conceive how a man could look up into the heavens and say there is no God.

We should, above all, be very grateful to Almighty God, who gives us victory.

I think I am a Whig; but others say there are no Whigs, and that I am an abolitionist.

Will you pardon me for asking what the horses of your army have done . . . that fatigue anything?

Never do anything for anyone who can just as well do it themselves.

If we do repel you by any wrong principle or practice, the fault is ours.

This country, with its institutions, belongs to the people who inhabit it.

I therefore consider that in view of the Constitution and the laws, the Union is unbroken.

Perfect relief is not possible except with time.

I do not believe any compromise, embracing the maintenance of the Union, is now possible.

The different parts of our country . . . [must] remain face to face; and intercourse, either amicable or hostile, must continue between them.

Stand fast to the Union and the old flag.

Your own resolution to succeed is more important than any other.

I am much indebted to the good Christian people of the country for their constant prayers and consolations.

You can't make a weak man strong by making a strong man weak.

Only those generals who gain successes, can set up dictators. What I now ask of you is military success, and I will risk the dictatorship.

Our reliance is in the love of liberty which God has planted in our bosoms.

I have not permitted myself gentlemen, to conclude that I am the best man in the country.

Our progress in degeneracy appears to me to be pretty rapid.

Shall the Union and shall the liberties of this country be preserved to the latest generation?

The written word may be man's greatest invention. It allows us to converse with the dead, the absent, and the unborn.

When the white man governs himself, and also governs another man, that is more than self-government—that is despotism.

And upon this act, I invoke the considerate judgment of mankind, and the gracious favor of Almighty God.

The mystic chords of memory will swell when again touched, as surely they will be, by the better angels of our nature.

Accustomed to trample on the rights of those around you, you have lost the genius of your own independence.

A nation may be said to consist of its territory, its people, and its laws. The territory is the only part which is of certain durability.

If they think they are able to slander a woman into loving them, or a man into voting with them, they will learn better presently.

Surely God would not have created such a being as man, with an ability to grasp the infinite, to exist only for a day!

Wanting to work is so rare a merit, that it should be encouraged.

Ballots are the rightful and peaceful successors to bullets.

We of this Congress and this Administration will be remembered in spite of ourselves.

I am struggling to maintain the government, not to overthrow it.

I have come to the conclusion never again to think of marrying.

Let every man remember that to violate the law is to trample on the blood of his father.

The sense of obligation to continue is present in all of us.

The workingmen are the basis for all governments, for the plain reason that they are the more numerous.

We can succeed only by concert. It is not, can any of us imagine better? But, can we all do better?

The world over, these are the thoughts at eventide when footsteps turn ever homeward.

When I have a particular case in hand, I love to dig up the question by the roots and hold it up and dry it before the fires of the mind.

If for this you and I must differ, differ we must.

You are ambitious, which, within reasonable bounds, does good rather than harm.

If we have no friends, we have no pleasure; and if we have them, we are sure to lose them, and be doubly pained by the loss.

Gen. Sheridan says "If the thing is pressed I think that Lee will surrender." Let the thing be pressed.

To correct the evils, great and small, which spring from want of sympathy, is one of the highest functions of civilization.

We must never sell old friends to buy old enemies.

We want those [democrats] who think slavery wrong to quit voting with those who think it right.

Kindness will wear well and will be remembered long after the prism of politeness or the complexion of courtesy has faded.

The love of property and consciousness of right and wrong have conflicting places in our organization.

I care not for a man's religion whose dog and cat are not the better for it.

Reduce the supply of black labor and you increase the demand for and wages of white labor.

When I so pressingly urge a strict observance of all the laws, let me not be understood as saying there are no bad laws.

Soldiers . . . I am greatly obliged to you, and to all who have come forward at the call of their country.

The books, and your capacity for understanding them, are just the same in all places.

Southern men declare that their slaves are better off than hired laborers amongst us.

If General McClellan did not want to use the army, he would like to borrow it.

From the first appearance of man upon the earth, down to very recent times, the words "stranger" and "enemy" were almost synonymous.

I am greatly obliged to you, and to all who have come forward at the call of their country.

Folks are usually about as happy as they make their minds up to be.

$\mathcal{I}$ am exceedingly anxious that this Union, the Constitution, and the liberties of the people shall be perpetuated.

$\mathcal{E}$ducation does not mean teaching people what they do not know. It means teaching them to behave as they do not behave.

$\mathcal{T}$o believe in the things you can see and touch is no belief at all—but to believe in the unseen is a triumph and a blessing.

$\mathcal{I}$f they decide to turn their back on the fire and burn their behinds, then they will just have to sit on their blisters.

I think that in such a case, to silence the agitator, and save the boy [soldier], is not only constitutional, but, withal, a great mercy.

*I*f we take habitual drunkards as a class, their heads and hearts will bear an advantageous comparison with those of any other class.

*N*othing stamped with the Divine image and likeness was sent into the world to be trodden on, and degraded, and imbruted by its fellows.

*S*o while we do not propose any war upon capital, we do wish to allow the humblest man an equal chance to get rich with everybody else.

Good things may come to those who wait, but only the things left by those who hurried.

Why should there not be a patient confidence in the ultimate justice of the people?

If I have made any assertion not warranted by facts, and it is pointed out to me, I will withdraw it cheerfully.

Let us diligently apply the means, never doubting that a just God, in his own good time, will give us the rightful result.

May I ask those who have not differed with me to join with me in the same spirit towards those who have?

I would to God that such a system [labor strikes] prevailed all over the world.

If you once forfeit the confidence of your fellow citizens, you can never regain their respect and esteem.

A duty to strive is the duty of us all. I felt a call to that duty.

Nearly all are educated—quite too nearly all, to leave the labor of the uneducated, in any wise adequate to the support of the whole.

The people themselves, and not their servants, can safely reverse their own deliberate decisions.

The better part of one's life consists of his friendships.

Are all the laws, but one, to go unexecuted,
and the government itself go to pieces,
lest that one be violated?

Still, let us not be over-sanguine of a speedy final triumph.

Jefferson had the coolness, forecast, and capacity
to introduce into a revolutionary document
an abstract truth.

I want every man to have the chance and I believe the
black man is entitled to it, in which he can better his
condition.

Love is the chain whereby to lock a child to its parent.

I have never denied the truth of the Scriptures; and I have never spoken with intentional disrespect of religion.

Every man's happiness is his own responsibility.

Resolve to be honest at all events; and if in your own judgment you cannot be an honest lawyer, resolve to be honest without being a lawyer.

Public opinion is founded on a property basis. What lessens the value of property is opposed, what enhances its value is favored.

I scarcely ever knew a mammoth farm to sustain itself; much less to return a profit upon the outlay.

I do not think much of a man who is not wiser today than he was yesterday.

The leading rule for the lawyer, as for the man of every other calling, is diligence.

Upon the subject of education, I can only say that I view it as the most important subject which we as a people can be engaged in.

My purpose is to be, in my action, just and constitutional.

I shall do more whenever I shall believe doing more will help the cause.

You think slavery is right and ought to be extended; while we think it is wrong and ought to be restricted.

Much disputation is maintained as to the best way of applying and controlling the labor element.

You are sure to be happy again. To know this, which is certainly true, will make you some less miserable now.

If you think you can you can, if you think you can't you're right!

I have here stated my purpose according to my view of official duty.

Nobody has ever expected me to be President.

They have not demanded of us to yield the guards of liberty in our state constitutions, but it will naturally come to that after a while.

I was losing interest in politics, when the repeal of the Missouri Compromise aroused me again.

I claim not to have controlled events, but confess plainly that events have controlled me.

I have always hated slavery, I think as much as any Abolitionist.

The things I want to know are in books.

And this too, shall pass away." How much it expresses! How chastening in the hour of pride! How consoling in the depths of affliction!

I now wish to make the personal acknowledgment that you were right, and I was wrong.

The highest art is always the most religious, and the greatest artist is always a devout person.

I have never spoken with intentional disrespect of religion in general, or any denomination of Christians in particular.

Neither let us be slandered from our duty by false accusations against us.

The Bible is not my book, nor Christianity my profession.

A woman is the only thing I am afraid of that I know will not hurt me.

I have found that when one is embarrassed, the shortest way to get through with it is to quit talking about it.

The mode is very simple, though laborious, and tedious. It is only to get the books, and read, and study them carefully.

Those who deny freedom to others deserve it not for themselves, and, under a just God cannot retain it.

Fortunately for the Union . . . it had a President who combined a logical intellect with an unselfish heart.

Peace is my companion on the pathway winding to the threshold.

It's not me who can't keep a secret. It's the people I tell that can't.

At what point then is the approach of danger to be expected? I answer, if it ever reach us, it must spring up amongst us.

These are only two roads to the same goal, and "popular sovereignty" is just as sure and almost as short as the other.

In this great struggle, this form of Government and every form of human right is endangered if our enemies succeed.

I am not bound to win, but I am bound to be true. I am not bound to succeed, but I am bound to live up to what light I have.

Of how little value the constitutional provision, if arrests shall never be made until defined crimes shall have been committed.

I still do not think any man has the right thus to insult the feelings, and injure the morals, or the community in which he may live.

I do not think I could myself, be brought to support a man for office, whom I knew to be an open enemy of, and scoffer at, religion.

All the good the Saviour gave to the world was communicated through this book. But for it we could not know right from wrong.

The ambition for broad acres leads to poor farming, even with men of energy.

When you have got an elephant by the hind legs and he is trying to run away, it's best to let him run.

The loss of enemies does not compensate for the loss of friends.

Give me six hours to chop down a tree and I will spend the first four sharpening the axe.

To the humblest and poorest amongst us are held out the highest privileges and positions.

Don't criticize them; they are just what we would be under similar circumstances.

With educated people, I suppose, punctuation is a matter of rule; with me it is a matter of feeling.

I take it that it is best for all to leave each man free to acquire property as fast as he can.

Plainly, the central idea of secession, is the essence of anarchy.

The struggle of today, is not altogether for today—it is for a vast future also.

$\mathcal{I}$ do not expect the Union to be dissolved; I do not expect the house to fall, but I do expect it will cease to be divided.

$\mathcal{I}$f there be in it any inferences which I may believe to be falsely drawn, I do not now and here, argue against them.

$\mathcal{I}$s there anything else that you think wrong, that you are not willing to deal with as a wrong?

$\mathcal{B}$etter to remain silent and be thought a fool than to speak out and remove all doubt.

$\mathcal{I}$mportant principles may and must be flexible.

Let every American, every lover of liberty, every well-wisher to his posterity, swear by the blood of the Revolution.

Better give your path to a dog, than be bitten by him in contesting for the right; not even killing the dog will cure the bite.

We have to hate our immediate predecessors to get free of their authority.

I can only say that I have acted upon my best convictions, without selfishness or malice.

Truth is generally the best vindication against slander.

Four score and seven years ago our fathers brought forth
on this continent, a new nation.

For the service you have done in this great struggle . . .
I present you sincere thanks for myself
and the country.

How miserably things seem to be arranged
in this world.

The best way to get a bad law repealed is
to enforce it strictly.

There can be glory in failure and despair in success.

It is the eternal struggle between these two principles — right and wrong — throughout the world.

That Kansas will form a Slave Constitution and ask to be admitted into the Union, I take to be an already settled question.

I am from home too much of my time for a young man to read law with me advantageously.

If you falter, and give up, you will lose the power of keeping any resolution, and will regret it all your life.

Labor is prior to, and independent of, capital.

You may drag my soul down to the regions of darkness and despair . . . but you will never get me to support a measure I believe to be wrong.

Too big to cry, too young to laugh.

I will prepare and some day my chance will come.

The best way to predict your future is to create it.

Still I am yet unprepared to give up the Union for a peace which, so achieved, could not be of much duration.

Now, that it could be said the war was over, the clamor against martial law, which had existed from the first, grew more furious.

Nothing valuable can be lost by taking time.

I laugh because I must not cry, that is all, that is all.

You know what a poor correspondent I am.

This extraordinary war in which we are engaged falls heavily upon all classes of people, but most heavily upon the soldier.

There seems ever to have been a proneness
   in the brilliant and warm-blooded to fall into
   this vice [drunkenness].

Let me close by asking three hearty cheers for
   our brave soldiers and seamen, and their gallant
   and skillful commanders.

No personal significance or insignificance can spare one
   or another of us.

There is a vague popular belief that lawyers are
   necessarily dishonest.

Public opinion in this country is everything.

That everyone may receive at least a moderate education appears to be an objective of vital importance.

The point you press—the importance of thorough organization—is felt, and appreciated by our friends everywhere.

I hate it [slavery] because of the monstrous injustice of slavery itself.

I believe the Bible is the best gift God has ever given to man.

Democracy will rise superior to the money power.

Again, a law may be both constitutional and expedient, and yet may be administered in an unjust and unfair way.

Labor is the superior of capital, and deserves much the higher consideration.

Free labor has the inspiration of hope; pure slavery has no hope.

I distrust the wisdom if not the sincerity of friends, who would hold my hands while my enemies stab me.

The time comes upon every public man when it is best for him to keep his lips closed.

What would be the effect upon the farming
   interest, to push the soil up to something near
   its full capacity?

An individual who undertakes to live by borrowing
   soon finds his original means devoured by interest.

Yield larger things to which you can show no more than
   equal right.

There can be no moral right in connection with one
   man's making a slave of another.

I shall do less whenever I shall believe what I am doing
   hurts the cause.

Every advocate of slavery naturally desires to see blasted, and crushed, the liberty promised the black man by the new constitution.

Character is like a tree and reputation its shadow. The shadow is what we think it is and the tree is the real thing.

The present moment finds me at the White House, yet there is as good a chance for your children as there was for my father's.

I go for admitting all whites to the right of suffrage who pay taxes or bear arms, by no means excluding females.

It has long been a grave question whether any government can be strong enough to maintain its existence in great emergencies.

To His care commending you, as I hope in your prayers you will commend me, I bid you an affectionate farewell.

An inspection of the Constitution will show that the right of property in a slave is not "distinctly and expressly affirmed" in it.

The South, flushed with triumph and tempted to excesses; the North betrayed, as they believe, brooding on wrong.

I do the very best I know how, the very best I can,
and I mean to keep on doing so until the end.

When the hour comes for dealing with slavery, I trust
I will be willing to do my duty though it cost my life.

Must I shoot a simple-minded soldier boy who
deserts, while I must not touch a hair of a wily
agitator who induces him to desert?

They did not make it so, but they left it so because they
knew of no way to get rid of [slavery] at that time.

The rudiments of science are available,
and highly valuable.

The occasion is piled high with difficulty and we must rise with the occasion.

Our strife pertains to ourselves . . . and it cannot be hushed forever with the passing of one generation.

Don't interfere with anything in the Constitution. That must be maintained, for it is the only safeguard of our liberties.

The job was a great national one; and let none be banned who bore an honorable part in it.

Let no feeling of discouragement prey upon you, and in the end you are sure to succeed.

If given the truth, people can be depended upon to meet any national crisis. The great point is to bring them the real facts, and beer.

We should never knowingly lend ourselves directly or indirectly, to prevent that slavery from dying a natural death.

May the Almighty grant that the cause of truth, justice, and humanity, shall in no way suffer at my hands.

However able and faithful he [a lawyer] may be in other respects, people are slow to bring him business if he cannot make a speech.

I have never had a feeling politically that did not spring from the sentiments embodied in the Declaration of Independence.

*W*hatever piece of business you have in hand, before stopping, do all the labor pertaining to it which can then be done.

*T*he [Patent Laws] secured to the inventor the exclusive use of his invention . . . adding the fuel of interest to the fire of genius.

*A*t least one of these important successes could not have been achieved when it was but for the aid of black soldiers.

We shall nobly save, or meanly lose,
the last best hope of earth.

The Republicans want to see all parts of the Union in
harmony with one another.

You cannot now believe that you will ever feel better.
But this is not true. You are sure to be happy again.

I have been driven many times upon my knees by the
overwhelming conviction that I had nowhere else to go.

Cast about and see if this feeling has not injured every
person you have ever known to fall into it.

I would rather be a little nobody, than to be an evil somebody.

Civilized belligerents do all in their power to help themselves, or hurt the enemy.

I remember my mother's prayers and they have always followed me. They have clung to me all my life.

The ant, who has toiled and dragged a crumb to his nest, will furiously defend the fruit of his labor.

In your temporary failure there is no evidence that you may not yet be a better scholar.

It is an old and a true maxim, that a "drop of honey catches more flies than a gallon of gall."

Don't worry, eat three square meals a day, say your prayers, and be courteous to your creditors.

I hold, that in contemplation of universal law, and of the Constitution, the Union of these States is perpetual.

As our case is new, so we must think anew, and act anew. We must disenthrall ourselves, and then we shall save our country.

Gold is good in its place, but living, brave, patriotic men are better than gold.

A jury too often has at least one member more ready to hang the panel than to hand the traitor.

Prohibition goes beyond the bounds of reason in that it attempts to control a man's appetite by legislation.

I fear it will be difficult for the world to understand how fully I appreciate the principles of peace.

The Constitution alludes to Slavery three times without mentioning it once! The language used becomes ambiguous, roundabout, and mystical.

I have always found that mercy bears richer fruits than strict justice.

Let reverence for the laws, be breathed by every American mother.

The power of hope upon human exertion, and happiness, is wonderful.

I am charged of maintaining the unity, and the free principles of our common country.

Everybody likes a compliment.

I have not pointed out difficulties, in order to discourage, but in order that being seen, they may be the more readily overcome.

The colored population is the great available and yet unavailed of, force for restoring the Union.

Peace does not appear so distant as it did. I hope it will come soon, and come to stay.

The old general rule was that educated people did not perform manual labor.

I do wish to see the spread of slavery arrested.

I believe the declaration that "all men are created equal" is the great fundamental principle upon which our free institutions rest.

Get a [law] license, and go to practice, and still keep reading.

I have no purpose, directly or indirectly, to interfere with the institution of slavery in the States where it exists.

These are not, however, the days of miracles, and I suppose it will be granted that I am not to expect a direct revelation.

For, whether we will or not, the question of Slavery is the question, the all absorbing topic of the day.

I do mean to say that bad laws, if they exist, should be repealed as soon as possible.

We the people are the rightful masters . . . to overthrow the men who pervert the Constitution.

Determine that the thing can and shall be done and then find the way.

This is a most valuable—a most sacred right— a right, which we hope and believe, is to liberate the world.

If there is anything that a man can do well, I say let him do it. Give him a chance.

Enough is known of Army operations within the last five days to claim our especial gratitude to God.

Every effect must have its cause.

Well, I wish some of you would tell me the brand of whiskey that Grant drinks. I would like to send a barrel of it to my other generals.

If you do not know it, you are inexcusable to assert it, and to persist in the assertion after you have tried and failed to make the proof.

By the "mud-sill" theory it is assumed that labor and education are incompatible; and any practical combination of them impossible.

I can make more generals, but horses cost money.

Suspicions which may be unjust need not be stated.

If those democrats think slavery wrong they will be much pleased when earnest men in the slave states take up a plan of emancipation.

I give thanks to the Almighty for this evidence of the people's resolution to stand by free government and the rights of humanity.

It is easy to demonstrate that "our Fathers, who framed this government under which we live," looked on Slavery as wrong.

Wherever slavery is, it has been introduced without law.

To sin by silence when they should protest makes cowards of men.

Here two will build new dreams—dreams that tomorrow will come true.

When the people rise in masses in behalf of the Union, truly may it be said, "The gates of hell shall not prevail against them."

Marriage is neither heaven or hell; it is simply purgatory.

You have confidence in yourself, which is valuable, if not an indispensable quality.

I feel just like the boy who stubbed his toe: too badly hurt to laugh and too proud to cry.

I don't know who my grandfather was; I am much more concerned to know what his grandson will be.

*A*ny policy to be permanent must have public opinion at the bottom; something in accordance with the philosophy of the human mind as it is.

*O*n the question of liberty, as a principle, we are not what we have been.

I appeal to all loyal citizens to maintain the honor, the integrity and the existence of our National Union.

Any people anywhere have the right to rise up, and shake off the existing government, and form a new one that suits them better.

Allow bygones to be bygones, and look to the present and future only.

If any man tells you he trusts America, yet fears labor, he is a fool.

The Presidency, even to the most experienced politicians, is no bed of roses; No human being can fill that station and escape censure.

Be not deceived. Revolutions do not go backward.

The world has never had a good definition of the word liberty, and the American people, just now, are much in want of one.

For we much prefer standing with old friends, to being driven to form new ones.

If I be right, the first thing is to get a just estimate of the evil; then we can provide a cure.

In view of this I think the time not unlikely to come when I shall be blamed for having made too few arrests rather than too many.

Elections belong to the people. It's their decision.

If there is anything that links the human to the divine, it is the courage to stand by a principle when everybody else rejects it.

The sooner the national authority can be restored; the nearer the Union will be to "the Union as it was."

Every man is proud of what he does well; and no man is proud of what he does not do well.

If elected I shall be thankful; if not, it will be all the same.

I have always thought "Dixie" one of the best tunes I have ever heard.

Let us consider the real case with which we are dealing, and apply to it the parts of the constitution plainly made for such cases.

I have always been in the habit of acceding to almost any proposal that a friend would make.

I could as easily bail out the Potomac River with a teaspoon as attend to all the details of the army.

Let not him who is houseless pull down the house of another.

Free Labor argues that it was probably intended that heads and hands should cooperate as friends.

In this time of national peril I would have preferred to meet you upon a level one step higher than any party platform.

Do I not destroy my enemies when I make them my friends?

We cannot but believe, that he who made the world still governs it.

The man who believes he can and the man who believes he can't; they're both right.

As a general rule, I abstain from reading the reports of attacks upon myself.

I hope to stand firm enough to not go backward,
and yet not go forward fast enough to wreck the
country's cause.

Prohibition makes crimes out of things that are
not crimes.

When I do good, I feel good. When I do bad, I feel bad.
That's my religion.

If in pain I wish to let you know it, and ask your
sympathy and assistance.

I confess I hate to see the poor creatures hunted down,
and caught, and carried back to their stripes.

It is the duty of people to never entrust to any hands but their own the preservation of their own liberties and institutions.

Some of you delight to flaunt in our faces the warning against sectional parties given by Washington in his Farewell Address.

You pulled that string as tightly as you could, but your very generous and worthy expectations were not quite fulfilled.

It is merely an ingenious falsehood, to degrade and brutalize the [black person]. Let each let the other alone, and there is no struggle about it.

If I could save the Union without freeing any slave I would do it, and if I could save it by freeing all the slaves I would do it.

Three fourths of mankind confess the affirmative with their tongues . . . the rest acknowledge it in their hearts.

We hoped for a happy termination of this terrible war long before this; but God knows best, and has ruled otherwise.

I expect to maintain this contest until successful, or till I die, or my term expires, or Congress or the country forsakes me.

I can never be satisfied with anyone who would be blockhead enough to have me.

The human instrumentalities, working just as they do, are of the best adaptions to His purpose.

Why is not an act dividing the territory as much against popular sovereignty as one for prohibiting polygamy?

I hate it [slavery] because it deprives our republican example of its just influence in the world.

You cannot lift the wage earner up by pulling the wage payer down.

The true rule, in determining to embrace, or reject anything, is whether it have more evil than of good.

I am for those means which will give the greatest good to the greatest number.

I wish not to be provoked by that to which I cannot properly offer an answer.

What I do about slavery, and the colored race, I do because I believe it helps to save the Union.

Democracy is the government of the people, by the people, for the people.

I fear explanations explanatory of things explained.

The brave men, living and dead, who struggled here, have consecrated it, far above our poor power to add or detract.

How can labor and education be the most satisfactory combined?

The man who stands by and says nothing when the peril of his government is discussed, cannot be misunderstood.

Much is being said about peace; and no man desires peace more ardently than I.

Avoid popularity if you would have peace.

Reason, cold, calculating, unimpassioned reason, must furnish all the materials for our future support and defense.

My great concern is not whether you have failed, but whether you are content with your failure.

I have lost every other friend on earth, I shall at least have one friend left, and that friend shall be down inside me.

If any man tells you he loves America, yet hates labor, he is a liar.

Whatever differs from this, to the extent of the difference, is no democracy.

Allow me to assure you that suspicion and jealousy never did help any man in any situation.

I am nothing, truth is everything.

I always plucked a thistle and planted a flower when I thought a flower would grow.

Before I talk to people, I spend two thirds of the time thinking what they want to hear and one third thinking about what I want to say.

Books, and your capacity for understanding them, are just the same in all places.

I say that the spread and strengthening and perpetuation of [slavery] is an entirely different proposition.

There are no accidents in my philosophy.

Be with a leader when he is right, stay with him when he is still right, but, leave him when he is wrong.

I will dwell on that no longer; I see the signs of the approaching triumph of the Republicans in the bearing of their political adversaries.

No administration, by any extremes can seriously injure the government in the short space of four years.

A tendency to melancholy . . . let it be observed, is a misfortune, not a fault.

Honor to the soldier and sailor everywhere, who bravely bears his country's cause.

It is no fault in others that the Methodist church sends more soldiers to the field than any.

God cannot be for, and against the same thing at the same time.

If the people should make it an Executive duty to re-enslave, I must be their instrument to perform it.

On principle I dislike an oath which requires a man to swear he has not done wrong.

I am most thankful if my labors have seemed to conduce to the preservation of the progress of the liberal arts.

Nothing is better known to history than that courts of justice are utterly incompetent to such cases.

The Lord prefers common-looking people. That is why he made so many of them.

In all matters but this of Slavery the framers of the Constitution used the very clearest, shortest, and most direct language.

The tribute to our noble women for their angel-ministering to the suffering soldiers, surpasses whatever has gone before.

Must a government, of necessity, be too strong for the liberties of its own people?

Towering genius distains a beaten path. It seeks regions hitherto unexplored.

I hope to stand firm enough not to go backward.

These slaves constituted a peculiar and powerful interest. All knew that this interest was, somehow, the cause of the war.

I have neither adopted, nor proposed any measure, which is not consistent with even your view, provided you are for the Union.

I have very earnestly urged the slave-states to adopt emancipation.

The little [work] he has done, comes to nothing, for want of finishing.

The ballot is stronger than the bullet.

I never had a policy; I have just tried to do my very best each and every day.

Men are not flattered by being shown that there has been a difference of purpose between the Almighty and them.

You can have no conflict, without being yourselves the aggressors.

Extemporaneous speaking should be practiced and cultivated.

Point out to them how the nominal winner is often a real loser—in fees, expenses, and waste of time.

We are guiltless of it, but our denial does not satisfy them.

In this sad world of ours, sorrow comes to all; and, to the young, it comes with bitterest agony, because it takes them unawares.

When you reach the end of your rope, tie a knot and hang on.

The only way to get rid of it [slavery] is, for those who think it wrong, to work together.

Things may come to those who wait, but only the things left by those who hustle.

Can it be persuaded that a particular drug is not good medicine for a sick man, because it can be shown to not be good food for a well one?

Now, I confess myself as belonging to that class in the country who contemplate slavery as a moral, social and political evil.

Slavery is the great political question of the nation. Though all desire its settlement, it remains the all-pervading question of the day.

It may seem strange that any men should dare to ask a just God's assistance in wringing their bread from the sweat of other men's faces.

May our children and our children's children to a thousand generations continue to enjoy the benefits conferred upon us by a united country.

I am a patient man—always willing to forgive on the Christian terms of repentance; and also to give ample time for repentance.

Our defense is in the preservation of the spirit which prizes liberty as the heritage of all men, in all lands, everywhere.

I desire a policy that looks to the prevention of [slavery] as a wrong; look hopefully to the time when as a wrong it may come to an end.

Labor is like any other commodity in the market; increase the demand for it and you increase the price of it.

No law is stronger than is the public sentiment where it is to be enforced.

And in the end it is not the years in your life that count, it's the life in your years.

He who molds public sentiment . . . makes statutes and decisions impossible to make.

No man has a good enough memory to be a successful liar.

Let them adopt the maxim, "Better luck next time;" and then, by renewed exertion, make that better luck for themselves.

The spirit which desired the peaceful extinction of slavery, has itself become extinct.

It will not do to investigate the subject of religion too closely, as it is apt to lead to infidelity.

I have understood well that the duty of self-preservation rests solely with the American people.

When I have friends who disagree with each other, I am very slow to take sides in their quarrel.

People who have no vices, have very few virtues.

Long experience has shown that armies cannot be maintained unless desertion shall be punished by the severe penalty of death.

The fiery trial through which we pass will light us down in honor or dishonor to the latest generation.

We can only speculate as to where that fault, that inadequacy, is, but we may perhaps profit by past experience.

The world will little note nor long remember what we say here, but it can never forget what they did here.

We will carry out the great work we have commenced.

Welcome, or unwelcome, agreeable, or disagreeable, whether this shall be an entire slave nation, is the issue before us.

I am sure that from such more elevated position, we could do better battle for the country we all love.

The strongest bond of human sympathy outside the family should be one uniting working people of all nations.

Don't worry when you are not recognized but strive to be worthy of recognition.

Hold on with a bulldog grip, and chew and choke.

If they stake their lives for us, they must be prompted by the strongest motive—even the promise of freedom.

All this talk about the dissolution of the Union is humbug—nothing but folly. We WON'T dissolve the Union, and you SHAN'T.

I do oppose the extension of slavery, because my judgment and feelings so prompt me.

I am pleased to know that, in your judgment, the little I did say was not entirely a failure.

If you make a bad bargain, hug it all the tighter.

The people can and will be furnished with a currency as safe as their own government.

The cause of these repeated failures is that our best and greatest men have greatly underestimated the size of this question (slavery).

The people will save their government, if the government itself will allow them.

Writing, the art of communicating thoughts to the mind through the eye, is the great invention of the world.

I don't like that man. I must get to know him better.

Being elected to Congress, though I am very grateful to our friends, for having done it, has not pleased me as much as I expected.

To us it appears natural to think that slaves are human beings; men, not property.

If friendship is your weakest point then you are the strongest person in the world.

Constituted as man is, he has positive need of occasional recreation.

• Nothing in this world is impossible to a willing heart.

We think slavery a great moral wrong, we wish to treat it as a wrong in the territories, where our votes will reach it.

I think the Democracy are pretty generally getting into a system of bushwhackery in this controversy.

You cannot keep out of trouble by spending more than your income.

A farce or comedy is best played; a tragedy is best read at home.

My conscience is my own—my creator's—not man's.

I freely acknowledge myself the servant of the people.

That slavery is right or wrong I suppose is the rub. It certainly is the only substantial difference between us.

The bare sight of fifty thousand armed, and drilled black soldiers on the banks of the Mississippi, would end the rebellion at once.

As I would not be a slave, so I would not be a master. This expresses my idea of democracy.

He has a right to criticize, who has a heart to help.

Every man is said to have his peculiar ambition.

If there be in it any statements, or assumptions of fact, which I may know to be erroneous, I do not, now and here, controvert them.

In this age, in this country, public sentiment is everything. With it, nothing can fail; against it, nothing can succeed.

We shall sooner have the fowl by hatching the egg than by smashing it.

Washington's is the mightiest name of earth—long since the mightiest in the cause of civil liberty.

One side will provoke; the other resent.

We trust, sir, that God is on our side. It is more important to know that we are on God's side.

The problem is too mighty for me. May God, in his mercy, superintend the solution.

The man of the highest moral cultivation, likes him whom he does know, much better than him whom he does not know.

Be sure you put your feet in the right place, then stand firm.

Life is hard but so very beautiful.

The successful application of steam power to farm work is a desideratum—especially a Steam Plow.

Can he [president] know the wants of the people, as well as 300 other men?

It will then have been proved that, among free men, there can be no successful appeal from the ballot to the bullet.

Everyone desires to live long, but none would be old.

Leave nothing for tomorrow which can be done today.

You can be anything you want to be, do anything you set out to accomplish if you hold to that desire with singleness of purpose.

There are those who are dissatisfied with me. To such I would say: You desire peace; and you blame me that we do not have it.

I know there is a God, and that He hates injustice and slavery.

Someday I shall be president.

All I have learned, I learned from books.

Hypocrite: The man who murdered his parents, and then pleaded for mercy on the grounds that he was an orphan.

Our government rests in public opinion. Whoever can change public opinion, can change the government, practically just so much.

This contrivance of a middle ground is such that he who occupies it is neither a dead or a living man.

If this country is ever demoralized, it will come from trying to live without work.

Quarrel not at all. No man resolved to make the most of himself can spare time for personal contention.

The slave-breeders and slave-traders, are a small, odious and detested class.

Choose some other occupation, rather than one in the choosing of which you do, in advance, consent to be a knave.

There are no bad pictures; that's just how your face looks sometimes.

It often requires more courage to dare to do right than to fear to do wrong.

There is no grievance that is a fit object of redress by mob law.

To give victory to the right, not bloody bullets, but peaceful ballots only, are necessary.

In giving freedom to the slave, we assure freedom to the free—honorable alike in what we give, and what we preserve.

The man who produces a good full crop will scarcely ever let any part of it go to waste.

Commitment is what transforms a promise into reality.

The people know their rights, and they are never slow to assert and maintain them, when they are invaded.

As president, I have no eyes but constitutional eyes; I cannot see you.

Even in times of peace, bands of horse-thieves and robbers frequently grow too numerous and powerful for the ordinary courts of justice.

To add brightness to the sun, or glory to the name of Washington, is alike impossible.

It is not best to swap horses while crossing the river.

Those who write clearly have readers, those who write obscurely have commentators.

The proportions of this rebellion were not for a long time understood.

If a house was on fire there could be but two parties, one in favor of putting out the fire, another in favor of the house burning.

Were it not for my little jokes, I could not bear the burdens of this office.

Nor must Uncle Sam's web-feet be forgotten. At all the watery margins they have been present.

A man watches his pear tree day after day, impatient for the ripening of the fruit.

Public sentiment is everything. With public sentiment, nothing can fail. Without it, nothing can succeed.

The one will taunt, the other defy; one aggresses, the other retaliates.

Broken eggs cannot be mended. I have issued the emancipation proclamation, and I cannot retract it.

I intend no modification of my oft-expressed personal wish that all men everywhere could be free.

If you are going to negotiate, don't let them talk you into fighting.

We hope all danger may be overcome, but to conclude that no danger may ever arise is dangerous.

Nations, like individuals, are subjected to punishments and chastisements in this world.

Did Stanton say I was a damned fool? Then I daresay I must be one, for Stanton is generally right.

We live in the midst of alarms; anxiety beclouds the future; we expect some new disaster with each newspaper we read.

We must ask where we are and whither we are tending.

It is better then, to save the work while it is begun.

A universal feeling, whether well or ill-founded, cannot be safely disregarded.

No client ever had money enough to bribe my conscience or to stop its utterance against wrong, and oppression.

I do not expect the house to fall—but I do expect it will cease to be divided. It will become all one thing or all the other.

Never let your correspondence fall behind.

Half-finished work generally proves to be labor lost.

By settling, you will likely get your money sooner, and with much less trouble and expense.

The Nebraska Law was conceived in violence, passed in violence, is maintained in violence, and is being executed in violence.

If my father's son can become President of these United States, then your father's son can become anything he wishes.

I am for no compromise which assists or permits the extension of the institution on soil owned by the nation.

I think we have fairly entered upon a durable struggle as to whether this nation is to ultimately become all slave or all free.

We never should be niggard of gratitude and benefaction to the soldiers who have endured toil, privations and wounds.

Consciousness of right or wrong have conflicting places, which often make a man's course seem crooked, his conduct a riddle.

I do, therefore, invite my fellow citizens to set apart and observe the last Thursday of November as a day of Thanksgiving.

By no advice or consent of mine, shall my pretentions be pressed to the point of endangering our common cause.

As a peacemaker the lawyer has superior opportunity of being a good man. There will still be business enough.

Why, when all desire to have this controversy settled, can we not settle it satisfactorily?

Human action can be modified to some extent, but human nature cannot be changed.

You cannot build character and courage by taking away people's initiative and independence.

I pray that our Heavenly Father may assuage the anguish of your bereavement.

It is easy to see that, under the sharp discipline of civil war, the nation is beginning a new life.

The privilege of creating and issuing money is the Government's greatest creative opportunity.

You cannot help people permanently by doing for them, what they could and should do for themselves.

The fourth of July has not quite dwindled away; it is still a great day for burning firecrackers.

I am not concerned that you have fallen—I am concerned that you arise.

Slavery extension is wrong; and out of the abundance of his heart, his mouth will continue to speak.

With high hope for the future, no prediction in regard to it is ventured.

Whoever rejects [constitutional checks] does of necessity fly to anarchy or to despotism.

In times like the present, men should utter nothing for which they would not willingly be responsible through time and eternity.

Nearly all men can stand adversity, but if you want to test a man's character, give him power.

I go for all sharing the privileges of the government who assist in bearing its burdens.

We never hear of the man who wishes to take the good of it [slavery], by being a slave himself.

Honest statesmanship is the wise employment of individual meanness for the public good.

I have desired as sincerely as any man that our present difficulties might be settled without the shedding of blood.

Republicans are for both the man and the dollar, but in case of conflict the man before the dollar.

To keep silent when we should protest, makes cowards of men.

I never had any faith, except a general hope that you knew better than I.

*W*hen the conduct of men is designed to be influenced, persuasion, kind, unassuming persuasion, should ever be adopted.

*B*eware of rashness, but with energy and sleepless vigilance go forward and give us victories.

I have neither assailed, nor wrestled with any part of the constitution.

*W*e are in civil war. In such cases there always is a main question.

You say you will not fight to free [black people]. Some
   of them seem willing to fight for you.

If we cannot give freedom to every creature, let us
   do nothing that will impose slavery upon
   any other creature.

Familiarize yourselves with the chains of bondage, and
   you are preparing your own limbs to wear them.

I have never studied the art of paying compliments
   to women.

Tact: the ability to describe others as they
   see themselves.

The legitimate object of government is to do for a community of people whatever they need to have done.

Go forward without fear, and with manly hearts.

Now we are engaged in a great civil war, testing whether that nation, or any nation so conceived and so dedicated, can long endure.

I appeal to all loyal citizens to favor, facilitate and aid this effort.

Posterity has done nothing for us.

Who can be more nearly a fiend than he who habitually overhauls the register of deeds in search of defects and put money in his pocket?

If I were two-faced, would I be wearing this one?

That some should be rich shows that others may become rich, and hence, is just encouragement to industry and enterprise.

This is what I call bushwhacking, a sort of argument that they must know any child can see through.

Suppose you go to war; you cannot fight, always.

I am glad to know that there is a system of labor where the laborer can strike if he wants to!

You can have anything you want if you want it badly enough.

Now I think it important that this matter [of slavery] should be taken up in earnest, and really settled.

The greatest fine art of the future will be the making of a comfortable living from a small piece of land.

These capitalists generally act harmoniously and in concert, to fleece the people.

How can anyone who abhors the oppression of [black people] be in favor or degrading classes of white people?

In your hands, my dissatisfied countrymen, and not in mine, is the momentous issue of the Civil War.

Freedom is not the right to do what we want, but what we ought.

Certainly it is not so easy to pay something as it is to pay nothing.

A capacity, and taste, for reading, gives access to whatever has already been discovered by others.

Force is all conquering, but its victories are short lived.

I shall try to correct errors when shown to be errors; and I shall adopt new views so fast as they shall appear to be true views.

Let's have faith that right makes might; and in that faith let us, to the end, dare to do our duty as we understand it.

One way to bring about a true settlement of the [slavery] question is to understand its true magnitude.

If I am killed, I can die but once; but to live in constant dread of it, is to die over and over again.

If slavery is not wrong, nothing is wrong.

If they should hang upon the gallows of their own building, I shall not be among the mourners of their fate.

If I were to read, much less answer, all the attacks made on me, this shop might as well be closed for any other business.

A human form with reason fled, while wretched life remains.

We fostered human slavery, and proclaiming ourselves, at the same time, the sole friends of human freedom.

The way for a young man to rise is to improve himself every way he can, never suspecting that anybody wishes to hinder him.

I was a little cross. I ask pardon. If I do get up a little temper I have no sufficient time to keep it up.

No man is good enough to govern another man without that other's consent.

We believe that the spreading out and perpetuity of the institution of slavery impairs the general welfare.

When the white man governs another man, that is more than self-government; that is despotism.

Let your military measures be strong enough to repel the invader, and not so strong as to harass and persecute the people.

You can tell the greatness of a man by what makes him angry.

We all declare for liberty; but in using the same word we do not all mean the same thing.

The most dumb and stupid slave that ever toiled for a master, does constantly know that he is wronged.

If you are going to fight, don't let them talk you into negotiating.

I have endured a great deal of ridicule without much malice; and have received a great deal of kindness, not quite free from ridicule.

Armies, the world over, destroy enemies' property when they cannot use it; and even destroy their own to keep it from the enemy.

You may fool all of the people some of the time; some of the people all of the time; but you can't fool all of the people all of the time.

We are not enemies, but friends. We must not be enemies. Though passion may have strained, it must not break our bonds of affection.

Let your military measures be strong enough to repel the invader, and not so strong as to harass and persecute the people.

You can tell the greatness of a man by what makes him angry.

We all declare for liberty; but in using the same word we do not all mean the same thing.

The most dumb and stupid slave that ever toiled for a master, does constantly know that he is wronged.

If you are going to fight, don't let them talk you into negotiating.

I have endured a great deal of ridicule without much malice; and have received a great deal of kindness, not quite free from ridicule.

Armies, the world over, destroy enemies' property when they cannot use it; and even destroy their own to keep it from the enemy.

You may fool all of the people some of the time; some of the people all of the time; but you can't fool all of the people all of the time.

We are not enemies, but friends. We must not be enemies. Though passion may have strained, it must not break our bonds of affection.

The Autocrat of all the Russians will resign his crown sooner than will our American masters voluntarily give up their slaves.

If a majority should deprive a minority of any clearly written constitutional right, it might justify revolution.

The taste is in my mouth a little; and this, no doubt, disqualifies me, to some extent to form correct opinions.

I am not at liberty to shift ground—that is out of the question. If I thought a repetition would do any good I would make it.

The human mind is impelled to action, or held in rest by some power.

Nowhere in the world is presented a government of so much liberty and equality.

I fear you do not fully comprehend the danger of abridging the liberties of the people.

The best thing about the future is that it comes one day at a time.

Slavery is founded in the selfishness of man's nature, opposition to it in his love of justice.

If you don't want to use the army, I should like to borrow it for awhile. Yours respectfully, A. Lincoln.

If people see the Capitol going on, it is a sign we intend the Union shall go on.

Let him attempt to force the ripening and he may spoil both the fruit and the tree.

Neither party expected for the war, the magnitude, or the duration, which it has already attained.

Moral principle is a looser bond than pecuniary interest.

The power confided in me will be used to hold, occupy, and possess the property and places belonging to the government.

We cannot avoid considering [slavery]; we can no more avoid it than a man can live without eating.

Let us have faith that right makes might, and in that faith, let us, to the end, dare to do our duty as we understand it.

In the haven of the hearthside is rest and peace and comfort.

Trusting in Him, who can go with me, remain with you and be everywhere for good let us confidently hope that all will yet be well.

Ready are we all to cry out and ascribe motives when our toes are pinched.

I am a success today because I had a friend who believed in me and I didn't have the heart to let him down.

Those who look for the bad in people will surely find it.

www.ingramcontent.com/pod-product-compliance
Lightning Source LLC
Chambersburg PA
CBHW061324040426
42444CB00011B/2757